Civic Skills and Values

Respect

By Dalton Rains

www.littlebluehousebooks.com

Copyright © 2024 by Little Blue House, Mendota Heights, MN 55120. All rights reserved. No part of this book may be reproduced or utilized in any form or by any means without written permission from the publisher.

Little Blue House is distributed by North Star Editions:
sales@northstareditions.com | 888-417-0195

Produced for Little Blue House by Red Line Editorial.

Photographs ©: Shutterstock Images, cover, 4, 6–7, 9, 10, 13, 15, 19, 21, 23, 24 (top left), 24 (top right), 24 (bottom left), 24 (bottom right); iStockphoto, 16

Library of Congress Control Number: 2022919845

ISBN
978-1-64619-820-7 (hardcover)
978-1-64619-849-8 (paperback)
978-1-64619-905-1 (ebook pdf)
978-1-64619-878-8 (hosted ebook)

Printed in the United States of America
Mankato, MN
082023

About the Author

Dalton Rains writes and edits nonfiction children's books. He lives in Minnesota.

Table of Contents

Respecting Others 5

Many Places 11

Other Ways 17

Glossary 24

Index 24

Respecting Others

Respect means you think about other people.
Then you act in a way that shows them you care.

It is important to respect your family.

They love you and want you to be happy.

When you listen to them, it shows respect.

You should be respectful to older people too. They have done many things in their lives. They have a lot to teach us.

Many Places

Respect matters in many places.

You can show respect in school.

You can listen in class.

People use the library to read and study.

They like it to be quiet.

You can show respect by staying quiet when you go there.

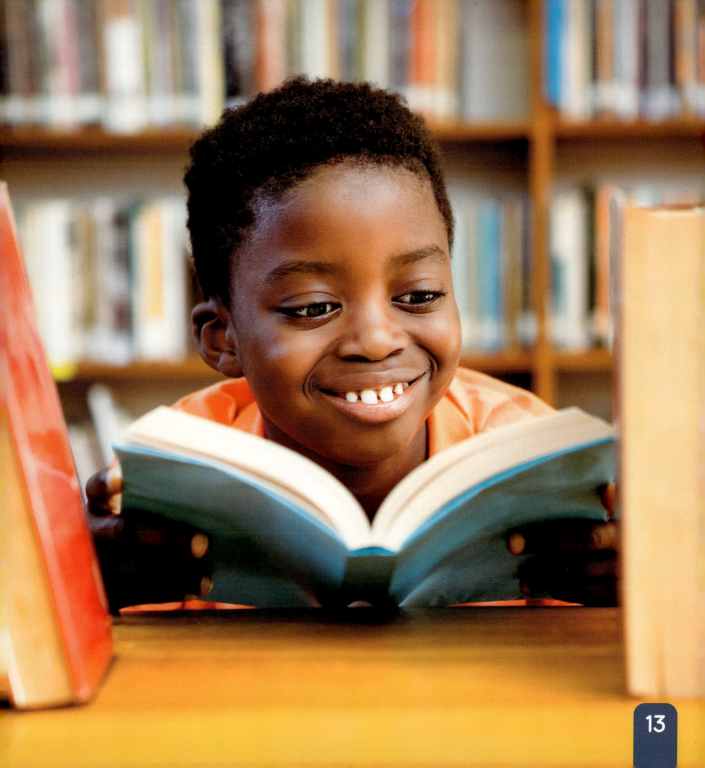

You can also respect the park.

Try not to make a mess.

Then others can have fun there too.

Other Ways

You can respect other people's things.

Your brother loves his toys.

You can be careful not to break them.

You can respect other people's space.
You wait in line for the bus.
You do not push or go in front of other kids.

You can respect other people's time. You get to the doctor early. Not being late shows respect.

Respect makes others feel good.

It shows that you care about them.

Glossary

bus

library

doctor

park

Index

C
class, 11

Q
quiet, 12

S
school, 11

T
toys, 17